How Are They Made?
Sweaters

Wendy Blaxland

Marshall Cavendish
Benchmark

New York

This edition first published in 2010 in the United States of America by
MARSHALL CAVENDISH BENCHMARK
An imprint of Marshall Cavendish Corporation

Website: www.marshallcavendish.us

This publication represents the opinions and views of the author based on Wendy Blaxland's personal experience, knowledge, and research. The information in this book serves as a general guide only. The author and publisher have used their best efforts in preparing this book and disclaim liability rising directly and indirectly from the use and application of this book.

Other Marshall Cavendish Offices:
Marshall Cavendish Ltd. 5th Floor, 32-38 Saffron Hill, London EC1N 8 FH, UK • Marshall Cavendish International (Asia) Private Limited, 1 New Industrial Road, Singapore 536196 • Marshall Cavendish International (Thailand) Co Ltd. 253 Asoke, 12th Flr, Sukhumvit 21 Road, Klongtoey Nua, Wattana, Bangkok 10110, Thailand • Marshall Cavendish (Malaysia) Sdn Bhd, Times Subang, Lot 46, Subang Hi-Tech Industrial Park, Batu Tiga, 40000 Shah Alam, Selangor Darul Ehsan, Malaysia

Marshall Cavendish is a trademark of Times Publishing Limited

All websites were available and accurate when this book was sent to press.

Library of Congress Cataloging-in-Publication Data

Blaxland, Wendy.
    Sweaters / Wendy Blaxland.
      p. cm. — (How are they made?)
    Includes index.
    Summary: "Discusses how sweaters are made"—Provided by publisher.
    ISBN 978-0-7614-4756-6
    1. Machine knitting—Juvenile literature. 2. Sweaters—Juvenile literature.3. Wool--Juvenile literature. I. Title.
    TT680.B54 2011
746.9'2--dc22

2009039882

First published in 2010 by
MACMILLAN EDUCATION AUSTRALIA PTY LTD
15–19 Claremont Street, South Yarra 3141

Visit our website at www.macmillan.com.au or go directly to www.macmillanlibrary.com.au

Associated companies and representatives throughout the world.

Copyright © Wendy Blaxland 2010

Edited by Anna Fern
Text and cover design by Cristina Neri, Canary Graphic Design
Page layout by Peggy Bampton, Relish Graphic
Photo research by Jes Senbergs
Map by Damien Demaj, DEMAP; modified by Cristina Neri, Canary Graphic Design

Printed in the United States

Acknowledgments
The author would like to thank the following for their expert advice: The Lance Armstrong Foundation, Austin, Texas, United States; Australian Wool Innovation, Sydney, Australia; Professor David Cottle, Sheep and Wool Science, School of Environmental and Rural Science University of New England, Armidale, NSW, Australia; Kendall Crolius, author of *Knitting With Dog Hair*, Southport, Connecticut, United States; Kaffe Fassett, artist, London, England; Icebreaker, Wellington, New Zealand; Professor Jim Johnston, University of Wellington, New Zealand; Betsy Lott, Mollywood Bird Sanctuary, Washington, United States; Colm McCarthy, The Aran Sweater Market, Inis Mór, Galway, Ireland; Dr Errol Wood, Lincoln Research Center, Christchurch, New Zealand.

The author and the publisher are grateful to the following for permission to reproduce copyright material:

Front cover photographs: Purple hoodie, Rob Cruse; stack of jumpers, Alle12/istockphoto (left) and (right).

Photographs courtesy of:
AAP/Photo Alto, **27** (right); AWTA, **18**; *Visit of the Angel*, from the right wing of the Buxtehude Altar, 1400–1410 (tempera on panel), Master Bertram of Minden (c. 1345–c. 1415)/Hamburger Kunsthalle, Hamburg, Germany/The Bridgeman Art Library, **6**; © Vincent Jannik/epa/Corbis, **25**; © Jack Fields/Corbis, **28**; © Peter M. Fisher/Corbis, **22**; © John Madere/Corbis, **17**; © Jacques Langevin/Sygma/Corbis, **20** (right); Rob Cruse, **3** (top), **8** (top), **11, 12, 23** (top), **29**; China Photos/Getty Images, **21**; Shannon Fagan/The Image Bank/Getty Images, **30**; Popperfoto/Getty Images, **24**; Wolf Suschitzky/Time and Life Pictures/Getty Images, **7**; Alle12/iStockphoto, **5** (bottom), **20** (left), **27** (left); Gary Alvis/iStockphoto, **8** (bottom); More Pixels/iStockphoto, **3** (bottom), **15**; © Cris Haigh/Alamy/Photolibrary, **4**; © Peter Wilson/Alamy/Photolibrary, **23** (bottom); © Phillip Quirk/Photolibrary, **9**; Phillipe P. Salia/Science Photo Library/Photolibrary, **19, 26**; © Robin Smith/Photolibrary, **14, 16**; © LWA Stephen Welstead/Photolibrary, **5** (top); Photograph by Rose Callahan, from the Winter 2008/09 issue of *Vogue Knitting* magazine, © SoHo Publishing Company, New York, **10**.

While every care has been taken to trace and acknowledge copyright, the publisher tenders their apologies for any accidental infringement where copyright has proved untraceable. Where the attempt has been unsuccessful, the publisher welcomes information that would redress the situation.

1 3 5 6 4 2

Contents

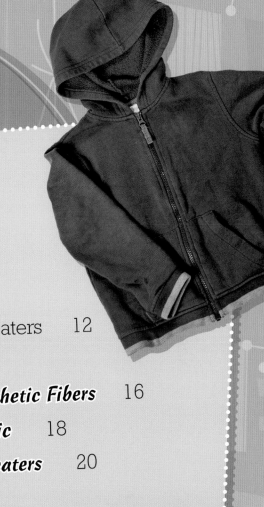

Glossary Words

When a word is printed in **bold**, you can look up its meaning in the Glossary on page 31.

From Raw Materials to Products

Everything we use is made from raw materials from Earth. These are called natural resources. People take natural resources and make them into useful products.

Sweaters

Sweaters are clothes that cover the body and arms. They protect these parts of the body and keep them warm. Sweaters are often worn over a shirt. Some are loose-fitting, while others fit closely. Hoods, belts, and decorations can be added.

The main raw materials for sweaters are wool and **synthetic fibers**, although other **natural fibers**, such as cotton, silk, and alpaca wool, are also used. Until synthetic fibers were developed, almost all sweaters were made of wool from sheep. Now most sweaters are made of synthetic fibers, or synthetics mixed with natural fibers. They can be hand-knitted or made from machine-knitted cloth.

Sweaters can be made from natural fibers, artificial fibers or a mixture of both.

Guess What!

In Britain and Australia, sweaters are known as jumpers, pullovers, or jerseys.

Whatever you choose—plain black
or richly colored patterns, political
slogans or sparkly decorations—
sweaters show who you are.

Why Do We Need Sweaters?

Sweaters mainly protect us from the cold. Sports sweaters can also shield athletes and adventurers from the sun and wind, or allow sweat to evaporate easily. Special sweaters made of very tough fibers protect police and the military from danger, while bright sweaters keep cyclists visible.

Sweaters often show membership of a group, such as a school or sports club. Players can be identified by names and numbers. Sponsors add their **logos** for advertising too.

Sweaters are also part of the fashion industry, and come in a huge range of colors, patterns, and styles. The sweaters people wear can reflect what they can afford, the way they feel, and their attitude toward life.

The History of Sweaters

Early sweaters were generally made of wool from sheep, one of the first tamed animals. Knitting may have grown from knotting **techniques** used for nets and spread by Arabian sailors. Our modern sweaters resulted from the tight-fitting fishermen's garnseys developed in Scotland and the Channel Islands. Now, new synthetic fibers are just as popular as wool in making sweaters.

This painting from 1390, by the German Master Bertram, is entitled The Knitting Madonna.

Sweaters through the Ages

6000 BCE
A tool called a spindle is used to twist fibers into thread.

3000 BCE
Sheep with a woolly fleece rather than hair are bred in what is now Syria, Turkey, Iran, and Iraq.

500–1000
The **spinning wheel,** possibly from China, is used in India.

Late 1500s
In England, jersey-style sweaters are knitted.

1589
Englishman William Lee develops a knitting frame. Panels can now be knitted instead of just tubes.

6000 BCE   3000 BCE   1 CE   500   1000   1500

3000 BCE–700 CE
The Nazca civilization in Peru develops a technique for making fabric by looping a single continuous thread on one needle.

300 BCE–700 CE
In Egypt, socks are made with a single-needle technique.

1100
Egyptian Copts develop the first true knitting using two needles, to make finely patterned cotton socks.

The patterns in Scottish fishermen's sweaters show where the sweater was made, because knitters from different places use particular combinations of stitches.

Question & Answer

What is a garnsey?

A garnsey is a Scottish fishermen's sweater, knitted tightly of greasy wool to keep out the cold and wind. Each village had its own designs of nets, ropes, and ladders, so sweaters might be used to identify a drowned fisherman's body.

1856
William Perkin invents the first synthetic dye.

1700s
The **Industrial Revolution** means textile workers move from home-based work in the country to city factories.

1939
Nylon is sold by the Du Pont company in the United States.

1953
Du Pont markets polyester.

1998
Biological harvesting of wool is invented.

1700

1800

1950

1975

2000

1700s
Scottish fishermen's wives knit elaborate patterns in sweaters for their men. By 1800, patterns are fixed.

1932
A shirt that **absorbs** sweat, called a sweater, is developed for a U.S. college football team.

1950s on
Sweaters become important casual wear.

July 1979
Sheep are first shorn by robot.

2000s
Sweaters are made of finer fibers so they begin to be worn alone.

What Are Sweaters Made From?

Guess What!

Many other natural fibers can be used to make sweaters. Cotton grows on bushes, silk is spun by silkworms, and cashmere is fine wool from goats. Yak and alpaca fleeces are also used to make wool for sweaters, as well as bamboo and even soybean fibers!

Sweaters are mostly made of wool from sheep, synthetic fibers such as polyester and nylon, or mixtures of wool and synthetics.

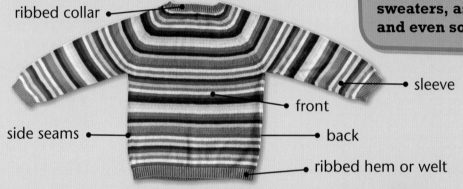

ribbed collar

sleeve

front

side seams

back

ribbed hem or welt

Cuffs, hems, and collars are made with a different stitch called ribbing to let them stretch and close again.

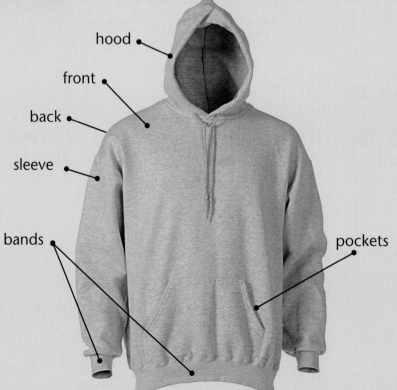

hood

front

back

sleeve

bands

pockets

Materials

Many different materials are used to make sweaters. As with the making of all products, energy is also used to run the machines that help shear the sheep, mine the oil for synthetic fabrics, and weave or knit the cloth.

Materials Used to Make Sweaters

Material	Purpose and Qualities
Wool	Made into **yarn** to be woven into sweater fabrics or hand-knitted into sweaters. Wool drapes well and repels water. It is hard to burn, long-lasting, easy to dye, and comfortable.
Polyester	The most commonly blended synthetic fiber, also used alone for fabric and thread. Polyester is strong, easily washable, and resists shrinking, stretching, and wrinkling.
Nylon	Used alone for fabric or blended with other fibers, nylon resists stains and is strong, smooth, comfortable, and easy to care for. Nylon **microfiber** feels, looks, and drapes like silk.
Cotton	Used alone or in blended fabrics, cotton is a warm, soft, long-lasting, absorbent, allergy-free material that breathes well. Cotton is also used as thread.
Dyes	Used to color yarn, fabric, and thread.
Buttons, feathers, fur, sequins, printing inks	Used in decorations.

Shorn wool. Only fine wool is used to make sweaters.

Guess What!

Some people even make sweaters with hair from their pet dogs!

Sweater Design

Specially trained designers create patterns for hand-made sweater **manufacturers**. They decide on a material, from fine **merino** wool, grown either in a conventional way or **organically grown**, to polyester, nylon, or a blended fabric that may also include cotton, hemp, silk, or even bamboo.

They must also decide:

✳ how heavy and stretchy the material will be

✳ the type of neckline, such as a V-neck, high-rolled turtleneck, or rounded crew neck

✳ the length of body and sleeves

✳ whether the sweater will be plain or decorated and what stitches and colors to use

✳ if and how it should be printed

✳ if the hem should have a border, such as ribbing or frills

✳ whether the sweater should have extra details, such as a hood or belt

Guess What!

Kaffe Fassett is an artist who has inspired people worldwide with his richly colored and patterned sweater designs. Kaffe learned to knit from a fellow passenger on a train.

This colorful zig-zag dress was designed by Brandon Mably, who works with Kaffee Fassett.

Hand-knitting is a creative and satisfying hobby that can be done almost anywhere.

Sweater Patterns

Knitters can buy pattern books, sometimes by well-known designers, or find patterns in magazines. Pattern books give instructions using shorthand terms that look strange to non-knitters. People who sew can also buy patterns for fabric sweaters, choose their fabric, and make up the sweater they want with individual decorations.

Unusual sweaters may include a variety of decorations, especially for holiday celebrations. These might use technology such as flashing lights or even pressure-operated sounds.

Guess What!

In the future, luxury woolen sweaters might be colored by minute particles, called nano-particles, of gold or silver embedded inside pure wool fibers. Researchers found that gold particles scatter light to give red, blue, and purple colors, while silver produces yellow, amber, and green.

From Wool and Synthetic Fibers to Sweaters

The process of making everyday objects such as sweaters from raw materials involves many steps. In the first stage, the wool is grown and shorn, and plastics are manufactured from **petrochemicals** and made into synthetic fibers. The second stage involves spinning the wool or synthetic fibers into yarn and weaving or knitting the yarn into cloth. In the final stage, the sweater is sewn together and decorated.

Stage 1: Growing Wool and Making Synthetic Fibers

Wool	Synthetic Fibers
The sheep are farmed to grow wool.	To make synthetic fibers, oil is first mined.
Then the wool is shorn from the sheep.	The oil is broken down into **polymers** at a **refinery**.
Next the wool is sorted.	The polymers are made into small plastic beads called nurdles.
It is packed into bales and sent to be sold to manufacturers.	

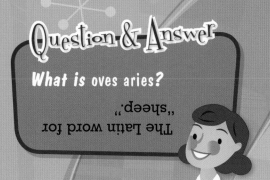

Stage 2: Making Yarn and Sweater Fabric

Wool is washed to remove dirt and grease.

↓

Then the wool is **carded** and combed to prepare it for spinning.

↓

Next, the yarn is twisted or spun to strengthen it.

↓

Then the yarn is wound onto **bobbins**.

↓

Finally, it is woven or knitted into cloth. Wool may be dyed at many points during this stage.

Nurdles may be dyed different colors. They are then melted and forced through tiny holes to produce long thin **filaments**.

↓

Then they are twisted into yarn ready for knitting or weaving.

Stage 3: Constructing and Finishing Sweaters

With hand-knitted sweaters, the front is sewn to the back and the sleeves to the body.

Sweaters made of woven fabric are first cut out in pieces according to the pattern.

↓

Then the front and back of the sweater are sewn together.

↓

Sleeves are given bands and joined to the sweater's body.

↓

Any extras, such as hoods, are added.

↓

Lastly, the sweaters may be decorated and a label added.

13

Raw Materials for Sweaters

Australia is the world's largest wool grower. Almost half of all wool used to make clothes, including sweaters, is Australian. This is partly because Australia has large empty spaces to raise sheep, though conditions are often very dry. Many other wool-producing countries such as South Africa, Argentina, and the Russian Federation have similar conditions. New Zealand, however, has a much higher rainfall and produces some of the finest merino wool for top-class fabrics, including sweaters.

Guess What!

A number of different types of sheep produce wool for sweaters. Saxon merinos are farmed in areas of high rainfall and are famous for their fine, soft wool. South Australian merinos live in very dry country and have the coarsest merino wool.

Australian sheep graze in a pasture.

NORTH AMERICA

United States of America

ATLANTIC OCEAN

Mexico

SOUTH AMERICA

Argentina

The Rise of Synthetic Fibers

Synthetic fibers have only been made for about fifty years, but they already account for half of all fiber production worldwide. Two-thirds of all synthetic fibers are made in the United States. Polyester is by far the most common synthetic fiber, followed by nylon.

This map shows countries that are important to the production of sweaters

Key

- 🐑 Important wool-producing countries
- 💧 Important oil-producing countries
- ✳ Important synthetic fiber-producing countries
- 🧶 Important wool-processing countries
- ⬆ Important sweater-manufacturing countries

Russian Federation 💧🐑

EUROPE

ASIA

United Kingdom 🧶
Poland ⬆
Germany ✳
Romania ⬆
Spain ✳⬆ Italy 🧶
Turkey ⬆🧶
Iran 💧
Saudi Arabia 💧
India 🧶
China 🐑💧✳🧶⬆
Japan 🧶
South Korea 🧶
Hong Kong ⬆
Vietnam ✳

PACIFIC OCEAN

AFRICA

South Africa 🐑

INDIAN OCEAN

Australia 🐑

ATLANTIC OCEAN

New Zealand 🐑

Stage 1: Growing Wool and Making Synthetic Fibers

The material that has been used longest for making sweaters is wool. Over the centuries, sheep have been bred for their wool.

Growing Wool

Sheep are raised in flocks on large grazing properties. In the spring, the farmer herds the sheep up to the shearing shed. A shearer cuts the sheep's fleece off in a set series of fast movements with electrical shears. The fleece is thrown onto a sorting table where the wool classer separates out the main fleece and supervises the packing into wool bales. These are sold by auction to the highest bidder.

Shearing is hard physical work.

Guess What!

Sheep can be shorn by robots! The sheep is clamped and turned while a robot quickly shears it. Using robots means shearers could work with less injury. The technique was developed in Western Australia in 1979, but lack of funds stalled the project in 1993.

Machines twist synthetic fibers into yarn to be woven or knitted into sweater fabric.

Making Synthetic Fibers

To make synthetic fibers, oil is first mined. The oil is then taken to a refinery and broken down into smaller molecules. Next these molecules are formed into long chains called polymers. This raw plastic is made into small beads, called nurdles.

The nurdles are melted or dissolved in special chemicals called solvents. They are then squeezed through tiny holes to produce long thin, filaments.

Question & Answer

How does biological sheep shearing work?

The sheep are fitted with a special net to hold the fleece together and given a protein that causes them to shed their wool. A week later, the fleece is removed by hand. This way sheep are not stressed by shearing and the fleece is of better quality.

Stage 2: Making Yarn and Sweater Fabric

Before being spun into yarn, wool is washed to remove dirt, sweat, and natural grease. Next, the wool is carded. Rollers covered with teeth tease the wool **staples** apart and lie them flat in a soft rope. The fibers are then combed to separate the long staples and lay them parallel, producing a combed sliver or "top." Several tops are blended, ready to be twisted together, or spun.

To make synthetic fibers ready for spinning, bundles of filaments are bent, then cut into shorter fibers so they can be blended with other materials.

Finally, fibers are spun by twisting them together to make a strong, long-lasting thread of yarn. The yarn is now wound onto a bobbin.

Wool may be dyed different colors at many stages, from loose wool to an entire garment. Synthetic fibers are generally dyed as nurdles.

Question & Answer

What is cashmere?

Luxurious cashmere sweaters are made of fine fibers from two or more cashmere goats. Cashmere is very soft, does not wrinkle, is cool in the summer, and warm in the winter. Cashmere sweaters become softer with age and may last a lifetime.

After being cleaned and carded, the soft ropes of wool are ready to be spun into yarn.

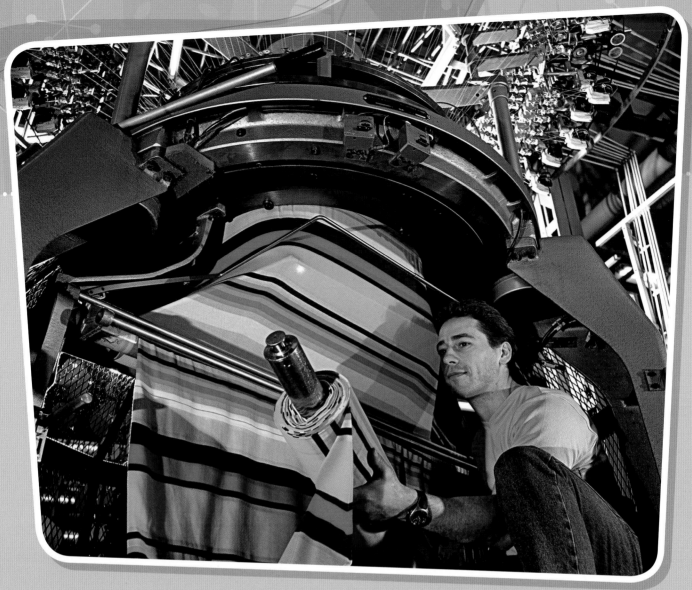

Making Sweater Fabric

The yarn is made into cloth by giant machines that weave a thread, called the weft, back and forth across a set of lengthwise threads, called the warp.

Synthetic yarn may be spun into polyester or nylon fabrics, or combined with wool, cotton, or other fabrics to create blended fabrics for sweaters. Microfiber fabric is made of very fine filaments of different synthetic yarns.

At the textile factory, numerous threads of yarn feed into this machine to be woven into fabric.

Hand-Knitting Sweaters

Yarn is hand-knitted into sweaters by using two or more needles to loop and lock a thread together. If two knitting needles are used, the free end of the yarn is held in the right hand and the other needle with the growing sweater in the left. Looping the thread in different directions and ways gives rise to different patterns. Traditional fishermen's garnseys were knitted without seams, using four needles.

From Wool and Synthetic Fibers to Sweaters
Stage 3: Constructing and Finishing Sweaters

If hand-knitted sweaters are knitted in pieces, the front must now be joined to the back by sewing and the sleeves sewn to the body.

Sweaters made of woven fabric, whether woolen or synthetic, are first cut in pieces the right size and shape according to the pattern. Often lasers, guided by computers, cut the fabric. Then workers use machines to sew the front and back of the sweater together, hem or band the sleeves, and join them to the body with a seam. Any hoods and pockets also need to be sewn on.

Workers sew the pieces of cashmere sweaters together at a factory in Mongolia.

Workers put the finishing touches on cashmere sweaters.

Finishing Sweaters

Some sweaters are made from printed fabrics. Others are decorated using special printing processes. Screen printing involves squeezing ink through fine holes in a screen onto the fabric and setting it with heat. Sweaters may also be printed with designs from a computer using special dyes and an inkjet printer. These designs are also set by heating.

Decorations can be sewn or embroidered onto the sweater, usually by machine, but sometimes by hand. Lastly, a label is sewn to the inside back of the sweater to give information about the size, manufacturer, fabric, and washing instructions. Then the finished sweaters are inspected for accurate sewing, clear printing, and tidy finishing.

Guess What!

One company making top-end woolen sweaters even adds a code on their labels so a buyer can trace on the website the actual sheep stations where the wool for his or her sweater was grown.

Packaging and Distribution

Products are packaged to protect them while they are being transported. Packaging also displays the maker's brand and makes products look attractive so people will buy them.

Sweaters made in factories are generally packaged in clear plastic bags to show their color and style while they are kept neatly folded. The bags may be printed with the manufacturer's label and other information about the product such as size and style. The sweaters are then packed in cartons and stored on pallets in warehouses until they are needed. Some warehouses are completely automated and do not even need lights.

Luxury and handmade sweaters are often either hung on coat hangers for display or folded without being put in plastic bags. Customers generally want to try these sweaters on.

Because sweaters are fashion items, people often compare a number of sweaters before choosing.

Question & Answer

What are bullet-proof vests and sweaters made of?

Bullet-proof garments are made from synthetic fibers called aramids, also known as Kevlar. These protective clothes for police, soldiers, and firefighters are lighter and tougher than steel.

Guess What!

Mini sweaters can keep birds that have lost their feathers warm, and improve the chances of fairy penguins surviving an oil spill.

Distribution

Most sweaters made in large factories are sent by rail, truck, or ship to where they will be sold. First they are sold to **wholesalers** who have the right to **distribute** the product in a certain area. Wholesalers then sell the sweaters to **retailers**, such as supermarkets, department stores, and specialist clothing stores, who sell them to individuals. Handmade sweaters may be sold in exclusive boutiques or souvenir stores.

Customers can also buy sweaters directly, either in markets or over the Internet, often to their own design. Retailers can buy directly from the manufacturer online too.

Sweaters from exclusive designers are often displayed separately.

Marketing and Advertising

Marketing and advertising are used to promote and sell products.

Marketing

Sweaters are fashion items, and fashion changes rapidly. Sweater styles reflect these changes, particularly advances in technology. Many brands emphasize the qualities of their fabrics, especially casual sweaters or those designed for energetic activities, such as mountaineering. Because wool is an expensive fabric, it is often marketed as a natural product instead of an artificial one. This appeals to people who prefer products made from sustainable resources. Younger customers, however, tend to buy sweaters because of the way they feel and how they perform, rather than the material they are made from.

Some sweaters in traditional patterns or styles are promoted to customers through the history behind the patterns.

Aran sweater designs have always been popular.

Guess What!

Aran sweaters have been knitted on the Aran Isles in Ireland only for the past one hundred years, but they are famous for their thick, naturally white, patterned wool.

Advertising Sweaters

Manufacturers often put their logo on sweaters, so that buyers are reassured about quality or can show everyone what brands they like or have the money to buy. Sweaters can show their wearers as being part of a group, such as soccer team supporters. Unusual sweaters may also demonstrate a person's individuality.

Sweaters are promoted directly through advertisements, and indirectly through being worn by people who are well-known or popular. Advertisements in newspapers and magazines include sweaters, but using catalogs to advertise sweaters is more common. The Internet is another way companies can advertise their sweaters, and allows small companies to have as big a presence as larger ones online.

Lance Armstrong wears the famous yellow jersey at the Tour de France. It is covered with advertising from race sponsors.

Production of Sweaters

Products can be made in factories in huge quantities. This is called mass production. They may also be made in small quantities by hand, by skilled craftspeople.

Mass Production

Clothing is big business, and sweaters are part of this. Most sweaters are made in large specialized factories, especially in China and other countries in Asia. These factories often use the latest technology and can produce huge numbers of the same style, which are sold worldwide. Much of the production of sweaters has shifted to these countries because costs are cheaper, particularly for labor. Some factories have modern equipment and treat their workers well. Others have less-safe working conditions than laws would allow elsewhere.

Some manufacturers use the latest technology to produce huge quantities of sweaters.

Small-Scale Production

Knitting sweaters by hand or machine is a satisfying hobby for many people. Knitting is easy to take with you, and can be done anywhere. Many people enjoy knitting on trains or while they watch television. Making a sweater for someone shows you are prepared to spend time and thought on them. Although knitting is often seen as a women's activity, there is also a long tradition of men as knitters.

Hand-knitted sweaters are a form of wearable art and making them is a satisfying act of creation. Wool for knitting comes in a huge variety of colors and textures, and sweaters can become treasured heirlooms.

Guess What!

The sleeves of very old Scottish fishing garnseys were often striped. When the cuffs began to unravel through long hard wear, they were reknitted, often with wool of a slightly different color.

Taking the trouble to hand knit a sweater is well worth the effort.

Sweaters and the Environment

Making any product affects the environment. It also affects the people who make the product. It is important to think about the impact of a product through its entire life cycle. This includes getting the raw materials, making the product, and disposing of it. Any problems need to be worked on so products can be made in the best ways possible.

Sustainable Materials

Natural fibers such as wool and cotton come from **renewable resources**. Some people, however, question whether the chemicals used in much cotton growing and in treating sheep for diseases can leave traces behind in the fibers. Most polyester and nylon comes from **nonrenewable** petrochemicals. Their manufacture contributes to global climate problems.

Working Conditions

Working conditions in sweater factories vary widely. Some factories are not always safe and do not pay fair wages. Nevertheless, conditions in many clothes factories are improving through campaigns for public awareness, fairer wages, and better working conditions.

Chemicals used in growing fibers, such as sprays to kill insects in cotton crops, may pollute the environment and the fibers.

*It can be fun and thrifty to find
vintage and recycled clothes.*

Recycling

A sweater is easy to recycle. If it is too small or you have grown tired of it, give your sweater away to someone else or to a charity store where it can delight another person as a bargain and also provide funds to help people. Even when old sweaters are too ragged to be worn any more, they can be used as soft rags for cleaning or in crafts. Some people make rag rugs from old fabrics, which can remind them of well-loved clothes, while being useful as well.

Guess What!

Sweaters can be fun. Why not have a winter party with an "ugly sweater" theme? Everyone wears the most unusual sweater they can find and then decides the winner. You can buy sweaters from second-hand stores.

Questions to Think About

We need to conserve the raw materials used to produce even ordinary objects such as sweaters. Recycling materials such as wool and synthetic fibers, conserving energy, and preventing pollution as much as possible means there will be enough resources in the future and a cleaner environment.

These are some questions you might like to think about:

❋ What is your favorite sweater? Why?

❋ Sketch a sweater you would like to make. What would you make it from and how would you decorate it?

❋ What are the advantages of wool as a material for sweaters?

❋ What are the advantages of synthetic fibers for sweaters?

❋ How can sweaters best be recycled?

Sweaters can keep you warm and comfortable, and they look great.

Glossary

absorbs
Is able to take in water.

biological harvesting
A method of shearing sheep in which sheep are injected with a substance that makes their wool fall off.

bobbins
Spools or reels used to hold thread.

carded
Brushed to untangle the fibers.

distribute
Sell a particular product.

filaments
Fine threads.

Industrial Revolution
Great changes in methods of production beginning in England in the 1700s.

logos
Images that represent company brands.

manufacturers
Makers, usually in factories with machines.

merino
Sheep breed valued for fine wool.

microfiber
Very fine threads of synthetic fiber.

natural fibers
Fibers from plants or animals, such as cotton or wool.

nonrenewable
Resources that cannot be easily replaced once they run out.

organically grown
Grown without the use of artificial fertilizers and pesticides.

petrochemicals
Chemicals made from petroleum oil or natural gas.

polymers
Long chains of molecules in substances such as plastic.

refinery
A factory where raw materials are treated to make them purer or more useful.

renewable resources
Resources that can be easily grown or made again.

retailers
Stores that sell products to individual customers.

spinning wheel
A machine that twists fibers into thread.

staples
Fibers of wool that have been graded for length and thickness.

synthetic fibers
Fibers such as nylon and polyester made by humans, often using petrochemicals.

techniques
Ways of doing things.

wholesalers
Businesses that buy very large quantities of goods and sell them to stores, rather than directly to individuals.

yarn
Thread made of fiber for knitting and spinning.

Index